THE HEALTH AND HAPPINESS HANDBOOK

Twelve weeks to a healthier YOU!

DANIELLE AITKEN

COPYRIGHT

Copyright © 2022 by *Project Heart Publishing*

Danielle Aitken

All rights reserved.

No part of this book may be used or reproduced by any means, graphic, electronic, or mechanical, including photocopying, recording, taping or by any information storage retrieval system without the written permission of the copyright owner except in the case of brief quotations embodied in critical articles and reviews.

The author and publisher have made every effort to contact copyright holders for material used in this book. Any person or organisation that may have been overlooked should contact the publisher.

NATIONAL LIBRARY OF AUSTRALIA
A catalogue record of this book is available from: www.trove.nla.gov.au

The Health and Happiness Handbook / Danielle Aitken

Editor: Julia Kaylock

Cover: Danielle Aitken

Interior design: Vellum

ISBN: 978-0-6488078-4-1(e)

ISBN: 978-0-6488078-5-8 (sc)

CONTENTS

The Health and Happiness Handbook	1
PART ONE	2
Why Create A Health and Happiness Handbook?	3
Neuroplasticity	7
Epigenetics	12
Let's Talk About Stress	15
What is mindfulness?	25
Gratitude	31
Meditation	37
Let's Talk About The Humble Breath	42
Conscious And Subconscious Awareness	48
The Power Of Thought	52
A Quote To Remember	55
You Are What You Think: Self-Fulfilling Prophecies	56
Your Solution State	63
Heart-Brain Coherence	69
PART TWO	72
Helpful Techniques And Daily Practices	73
Breath Techniques and Practices	74
Practices to Enhance Neuroplasticity	82
Mindful Practices	91
Daily Meditation Practices	100
Your Thoughts Are Powerful	105
Creating Your Solution State	110
Daily Gratitude Practices	114
Afterword	117
About the Author	119
Also by Danielle Aitken	121
"BELIEVE AND YOU WILL ACHIEVE"	122
References	123

THE HEALTH AND HAPPINESS HANDBOOK

Twelve weeks to a healthier you!
Change happens because of what you do in THIS moment

Danielle Aitken.

Counsellor, Clinical Hypnotherapist, R.N.,R.M.
National President Australian Hypnotherapists' Association

PART ONE

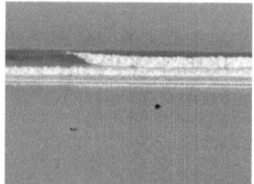

Knowledge and understanding are the catalysts to creating change.

Let's start learning

The moment you become 'aware' of anything, be it a thought, feeling or behaviour, you are immediately in a position of choice.
What you choose in that moment will determine your outcomes.

WHY CREATE A HEALTH AND HAPPINESS HANDBOOK?

This handbook and the accompanying **companion journal** are purposefully designed to give you, the reader, specific tools, and information to help create meaningful, and solution-focused changes to your life.

In my daily work I help clients uncover their potential to be all that they can be. Assisting them to commence a journey of self-discovery through mindful awareness begins with identifying the ineffective practices that have been holding them back.

The aim of this handbook is to demonstrate scientifically-based techniques to create positive change in *your* life; by overcoming the mechanisms that have been responsible for keeping you stuck in old self-defeating patterns and routines, and by providing effective therapeutic tools and techniques, with which to connect to your inner potential to heal both mind and body.

Many physical and emotional issues and health concerns, such as anxiety, depression and even inflammation, to name a few, can be markedly improved just by looking at the patterns and habits you are unwittingly creating with your thoughts, feelings, beliefs, and repetitive behaviours each and every day.

The key word here is *'unwittingly'*. This statement is not about blame; it is about taking responsibility. When you begin to entertain the concept that you have more influence over your immediate outcomes than you ever dreamed possible, you become empowered to create potent changes in your life.

This is your birthright, your potential, your choice.

I wonder if you have ever noticed that those same worrying or upsetting thoughts that you focus on, or ruminate over last thing at night, the ones that are probably preventing a good night's sleep, are often the very same thoughts and feelings that immediately spring to mind the moment you open your eyes in the morning. The truth is, when you continue to re-run unhelpful programs focusing on yesterday's problems, issues, or mistakes, you are effectively dragging yesterday, with all its limitations and disappointments, into today, recreating it in this moment when none of it is probably happening.

As a mental health practitioner and advocate, I find myself very often repeating the same therapeutic advice. No matter what the presenting issues have been, most clients have found that by making small but significant changes to their daily practices, in the ways described in this handbook, they have finally taken back the control of their lives.

∼

The practices described within the pages of this handbook are simple, yet complex at the same time. Practices that are based on the positive benefits of cognitive therapies, gratitude, and mindfulness mixed with a touch of physiology, neuroplasticity, epigenetics and a sprinkle of quantum physics. Together these have been shown to be helpful in changing our mindset and improving our physical state of wellbeing, but please, don't be afraid of these terms. Your body already knows what to do, you just have to start giving it a different set of instructions. This is the gift you were meant to give to yourself, to create the life you choose to live.

I have personally used these techniques and have changed *my* life in many powerful ways; healing both mind and body, and I have seen many others do the same. On my own journey I have learned a great deal about what works and what doesn't, when it comes to mental and physical wellbeing. The knowledge I have gained through my own self-healing, as well as through my observations of the empowered endeavours and results of my clients, is combined with evidence-based practices that will be discussed in this handbook, providing *you* with easy tools and techniques that can make a significant difference to your daily experience.

What this all means is that ordinary people can, and do, achieve extraordinary outcomes, when they know how, and just as importantly, when they believe they can!

If I can do this, and if they can do this, you can too.

This handbook is written in such a way that you can open it anywhere and gain benefit from the information and evidence-based practices displayed on every page.

DANIELLE AITKEN

Some of you may choose to read it from cover to cover; others may choose to select the topics most relevant to themselves.

So, let's begin!

NEUROPLASTICITY

I begin with neuroplasticity because this is your key to unlocking the changes you desire, and it is of vital importance when it comes to getting rid of old and ineffective habits, patterns of behaviour, and even thought processes.

I am not asking you to become a neuroscientist, but put simply, your brain already knows all about change, and when you learn to connect to this ability, by speaking the language your body understands, you can be assured of some empowered outcomes.

When I began nursing back in the unenlightened days of the early 1980's, we were taught that the brain was the most important organ of the body, and if we injured this precious organ there was little, or no chance, of any neural regeneration – no functional ability to rewire, heal or create change.

We were told that our brain cells were dying, almost from the moment of birth, and that risk-taking behaviours such as having an alcoholic drink, or even holding our breath for extended periods of time, would mean certain death to a finite number of precious brain cells.

Even before I started nursing, I was imbued with this misinformation from a very early age. When I think back, I can remember often trying to outdo a friend or sibling by attempting to swim the furthest underwater, generally coming up gasping for air, whilst somewhere in the back of my mind I was having the guilty thought that I had just knocked off a few more brain cells. Combine this with the normal 'after work activities' of so many young nurses, I think it was fair to say that 'neurologically' things were looking pretty grim.

Fast forward forty years and thank goodness, science has now caught up with what the body has always known, that nothing could be further from the truth. Like so many other advances in scientific research and medical knowledge, this old paradigm came to an abrupt but timely end.

Welcome the birth of the science and study of neuroplasticity and epigenetics.

WHAT IS NEUROPLASTICITY?

Neuroplasticity refers to the brain's ability to change its structure and function as it adapts to new experiences and to new sensory input. What this means is that the brain has the ability to rewire and reorganise itself in response to injury, or new situations.

When this happens, a process called 'neural sprouting' allows for new neural connections, creating new 'neural pathways', whilst another process called 'neural pruning' occurs simultaneously in other areas of the brain, effectively decommissioning old or redundant neural pathways. This is how we change outdated habits and we can use this same principal to help create the changes you desire.

I'm sure you have all heard the saying, 'if you don't use it, you lose it'. Well, neurologically this is true.

WHAT IS A NEURAL PATHWAY?

To put it simply, a neural pathway is a collection of brain cells that have wired together to run a specific function in the body, be it a habit, behaviour, an emotional reaction, recurrent thoughts, or even recurrent feelings. Your repetitive focus of attention or repetition of the behaviour keeps it firing and wiring.

. . .

HOW CAN NEUROPLASTICITY WORK FOR YOU?

Although neuroplasticity is a completely natural function of the brain that is occurring all the time, we now also know that you can intentionally influence your own neural activity to design your desired outcomes. By deliberately practicing certain cognitive functions and neuroplasticity exercises presented in this handbook, you can stimulate neural activity with specific outcomes in mind. Repetitive practices and focused attention will strengthen new neural pathways, which leads us to Hebb's Rule, postulated by Donald Hebb in 1949: ***Neurons That Fire Together Wire Together***

Those of us wishing to create new changes in our lives need to constantly fire, or run, our desired programs, making them the new dominant pathways. Repetition and practice are vital for the strengthening of these new neural pathways, which will lead to our ability to change the habits and behaviours that are no longer serving us.

Living in the country, I often use the analogy of a cow track in the paddock to describe this phenomenon to my clients.

> *If one cow walks through the paddock, you can sometimes notice a slight parting of the grass, making you aware that an animal has walked that way. If ten cows walk that same path, the grass begins to flatten and the path is more visible, but when a herd of cows walks the same path twice a day to the milking shed, the path becomes larger and more permanent. However, if the cows stop using it, that same path will soon become decommissioned, overgrown with grass and disappear from sight.*

The traffic the path receives, therefore, determines if it stays or goes. Neural pathways work in a similar way.

Many of the techniques described in this handbook are designed to interrupt old patterns of thinking and feeling, thus creating new neural pathways so you can begin to live the life you desire. However, it is important to remember the cow track analogy here. When you start to feel better, if you stop doing the things that made you feel better in the first place, *your* new pathways will also be decommissioned, and you may find yourself reverting to old habits, patterns, and behaviours.

Disrupting old patterns and creating new neural pathways requires daily practice.

Please refer to Part Two, **Helpful Techniques and Daily Practices**: *Neuroplasticity Techniques* for ways to help rewire your brain for different responses.

EPIGENETICS

WHAT IS EPIGENETICS, AND HOW CAN THIS WORK FOR YOU?

Epigenetics is the study of the mechanisms that turn gene expression on and off.

We have always known that our genes play a pivotal part in our health outcomes, but here's the good news: so do our behaviours, our thoughts, and specific environmental factors!

The moment you have any thought, your body immediately responds by releasing hormones straight into your bloodstream. These chemical messengers have a direct effect on your internal environment at a cellular level, which instantly bathes your cells in a cocktail of chemicals and hormones directly related to your specific thought. This is highly beneficial for your health and wellness, as long as your thoughts are those of love, compassion and gratitude. However, if your thoughts make you feel anxious, angry or depressed, the hormones immediately released into your body will be stress chemicals such as adrenaline, norepinephrine and cortisol. Naturally the long-term effects of bathing your internal environment at a cellular level with these stress hormones will not be beneficial.

If the latter is your habit, over time these stress chemicals will have a damaging effect on your body, negatively affecting your gene expression at a cellular level; they may even create the exact situation that you have been worrying about in the first place.

So, to be absolutely clear, the internal environment that *you* create with *your* thoughts *will* impact on your genetic expression. In simple terms, what this means is that although we can't change our genes, we can influence the expression of them via the environmental signals coming in, which regulate them, resulting in gene expression either turning on or turning off. Thus, as I will discuss later in this handbook, your focus of attention is very important to your health outcomes, both emotionally and physically.

The important message here is that we are not doomed to be lifelong recipients of an inescapable or ill-fated gene pool. While genetics will certainly influence your predisposition to certain disorders, environmental factors such as life experiences, grief and loss, or other life stressors also play their part.

External factors also impact upon gene expression, and although we may not be able to control what is happening around us, we can always control how we respond to these things.

What this means is that we *can* influence what happens to us on a genetic level, and that is exciting!

Put simply
You are not your genes!

LET'S TALK ABOUT STRESS

WHAT IS STRESS?

There are many definitions for stress, such as:

'The reaction people may have when presented with demands and pressures that are not matched to their knowledge and abilities, and which challenge their ability to cope'

Ref: World Health Organisation

OR

'A state of mental or emotional strain or tension resulting from adverse or demanding circumstances'

Ref: Oxford Languages Dictionary

I'm sure each reader will have their own understanding of what stress is, especially if they have been adversely affected by situations in their life that have been hard to deal with. And although stress is *not* a disease, it certainly causes disease to every system in the body, if left unchecked. Stress has been dubbed 'the health epidemic of the 21st Century' by the World Health Organisation, so however we define it, it is imperative that we learn effective strategies to deal with it, because stress is an inevitable part of life, and it isn't going anywhere anytime soon.

STRESS MODE:
What is it?

Activation of the **Sympathetic Nervous System** is often referred to as *'Fight-Flight-Freeze Mode'* or *'Stress Mode'*. For the purpose of this discussion, I will be calling it **'fight-flight mode'** because the sudden release of chemicals that occurs during this state prepares the body to either run away from impending danger or fight to defend itself.

The interesting thing about fight-flight mode is that human beings are the only species in the world who can very effectively turn on this chemical and physical response in a millisecond, just with a thought, in the complete absence of any real danger. In fact, many of us live in 'stress mode' for a majority of the time, existing in a generalised state known to most as anxiety.

For many, this mode is triggered by worry: about the deadline that is looming, the phone call we need to make, the email we haven't read or replied to, the exam we are about to sit, or any number of other normal day-to-day experiences.

Beyond Blue estimates that at any given time in Australia two million people are living with diagnosed anxiety, and I would postulate that quite probably there are many more who remain undiagnosed.

When this state becomes our 'normal', physical changes begin to occur in the brain to accommodate the stress chemicals and stress feelings we continue to turn on with our thoughts. The brain's stress centre, the amygdala, adjusts to the 'stressed state' by becoming enlarged, while simultaneously, other areas of the brain shrink.

The hippocampus, the area of the brain that stores memories, and the prefrontal cortex, the area that deals with making decisions, working memory and impulse control are both reduced in size during prolonged stress. If that is not enough to get your attention, stress also kills existing brain cells and slows regeneration of new brain cells. These changes effectively wire the brain for stress and a new base line is created.

Being 'stressed-out' becomes our normal, we may even take ownership of this state by saying *'I am an anxious person'* or *'I'm always stressed'*. This becomes a self-fulfilling prophecy, because the more we feel stressed, the more stressed thoughts we have, and the more stressed thoughts we have the more we feel stressed – in a never-ending loop.

This is probably a good time to reflect on the principles of neuroplasticity, as we remember 'Hebb's Rule': *Neurons that fire together, wire together.* Thus, the longer you linger in the state of anxiety, worry, fear or any other emotion that triggers activation of your fight-flight mode, the more you are wiring your brain for these states.

Now please don't get me wrong, fight-flight mode is a wonderful bodily response that you really want to kick into action, automatically and immediately, when there is a *real* danger, such as if you were to place your hand on a hotplate, or step in front of a bus. But we are not supposed to *live* in fight-flight mode; to do so puts *an increased chemical and physical load on the body,* **known as an allostatic load,** the effects of which cause emotional and physical damage.

To reinforce the wisdom of actively reducing your allostatic load, I can tell you that an increased allostatic load has been linked to:

- cardiovascular disease
- hypertension (high blood pressure)
- wear and tear on the peripheral vascular system (veins and arteries)
- increased anxiety and depression
- increased psychological disorders
- higher levels of self-rated 'stress'
- weight gain
- higher blood glucose levels
- increased risk of diabetes
- lower bone density
- fibromyalgia
- body aches and pains
- increased frailty
- impaired cognitive function
- reduced memory
- cognitive decline

An increased allostatic load is connected to poor health outcomes, so you are hopefully beginning to agree that it is a prudent idea to reduce your allostatic load as soon as possible.

The techniques presented in this handbook are designed to do just that.

Please refer to Part Two, **Helpful Techniques and Daily Practices:** *Practices to Enhance Neuroplasticity* for ways to help rewire your brain for different responses.

WHAT ARE THE NEGATIVE EFFECTS OF PROLONGED STRESS?

The effects of prolonged stress due to inappropriate activation of fight-flight mode can be physical, emotional and/or behavioural.

PHYSICAL EFFECTS:

- a surge in chemicals in the body to manage the non-existent threat
- thick sticky blood; ready to clot if you are injured
- high blood lipids/fats, leading to high blood glucose levels
- high blood glucose – so you can fight or run
- increased and/or shallow breathing
- increased heart rate
- increased wear and tear on the circulatory system due to chemical changes
- increased hardening of the arteries leading to;
- high blood pressure
- increased risk of stroke and heart attack
- blood is diverted away from skin/gastrointestinal tract leading to;
- visible aging
- digestive issues such as nausea, constipation, indigestion, irritable bowel

- prolonged brain exposure to neurotoxic stress chemicals leading to:
- damaged brain cells over time and increased predisposition to dementia
- reduced neurogenesis; the creation of new brain cells
- thinning of grey matter leading to decreased processing and clarity of thought
- reduced function of the immune system
- reduced function of the reproductive system
- increase muscle pains
- increased inflammation
- rapid ageing of our DNA associated with 'telomere' shortening
- increase in size and function of the brain's stress centre due to over-activation, thus the brain rewires itself, ready for more stress.

EMOTIONAL AND BEHAVIOURAL EFFECTS:

- increased anxiety
- increased depression
- increased alcohol and drug abuse
- irritability
- anger outbursts
- increased domestic violence
- increased anti-social behaviours
- isolation
- restlessness
- feelings of overwhelm
- increased relationship issues
- insomnia
- rumination.

PROLONGED STRESS EFFECTS EVERY SYSTEM OF YOUR BODY!

- *your cardiovascular system:* making it more likely that you will have a heart attack, stroke, high blood pressure, increased heart rate and thicker blood.
- *your central nervous system:* over activation of your sympathetic nervous system leads to damaging brain changes.
- *your respiratory system:* breathing rate often increases and becomes shallow. Oxygen is sent to the extremities to fight or run. Resulting hyperventilation can lead to a feeling of 'panic'.
- *your endocrine system:* stress hormones are released, causing damage to the body over time (increased allostatic load).
- *your immune system:* high circulating stress chemicals weaken the immune system, creating damage to certain cells, often leading to chronic inflammation over time. These damaging changes make you more susceptible to infections and disease.
- *your musculoskeletal system:* chronic stress leads to tension in the body often resulting in muscle tightness, aches, pains, and fatigue.
- *your gastrointestinal system:* all bodily resources are redirected away from the digestive tract during stress, therefore digestive upsets are very common.
- *your integumentary system:* this is your skin, nails and hair. All of these are affected over time as stress mode redirects needed resources away from these areas.
- *your reproductive system:* the effects of circulating stress chemicals in the body reduce the functioning of

the reproductive system, as all non-essential functions are reduced in fight-flight mode.

That's the bad news, however, the good news is, **if you can put your body into stress mode in an instant with your thoughts –** *and you can* – then perhaps you are beginning to recognise that it is possible to turn off stress mode in the same way.

The good news is not only is it possible to turn off stress mode and reduce the allostatic load your body has been dealing with; it is also possible to **rewire your brain for more calm and more positivity** in as little as six to twelve weeks.

The steps are simple and will be described in Part Two, **Helpful Techniques and Daily Practices**. Success, however, requires the same persistence and repetition that caused the problem state in the first place, and awareness is the key.

The moment you become aware of anything; you are immediately in a position of choice. What you choose in that moment will determine your outcomes.

The body is complex, that is true, however when we learn to speak to it in a language that it understands, we can instantly create calm and clarity.

To reduce stress, please refer to Part Two, **Helpful Techniques and Daily Practices**: *Practices to Enhance Neuroplasticity / Mindful Practices / Your Thoughts are Powerful / Breath Techniques and Practices*

MINDFULNESS

WHAT IS MINDFULNESS?

Jon Kabat-Zinn; Professor of Medicine Emeritus, University of Massachusetts Medical School and founding director of the Mindfulness-Based Stress Reduction program, has defined the practice of mindfulness to be:

The awareness that arises from
paying attention ,**on purpose,**
in the present moment,
non-judgementally.

There are three key elements identified in the practice of mindfulness.
These include states of being:

Aware
Non-judgemental
Non-reactive

"YOU CAN'T STOP THE WAVES BUT YOU *CAN* LEARN TO SURF"

I love this quote by **Jon Kabat-Zinn.**

To me it says so much about surrendering the struggle of trying to control the things we cannot control, and instead choosing to go with the flow into an ocean of new possibilities.

WHY CHOOSE MINDFULNESS?

When I choose to be mindful, I am choosing to let go of the 'should-haves', 'could-haves' and the 'if only's' of the past, and the 'what if's' of the future, turning my attention instead to the present; observing the 'here and now' as it unfolds, moment by moment.

What this means for me, is that I can enjoy what is happening in the present moment, because this is, in fact, the only moment we have. The past no longer exists. It is, however, a source of wisdom, knowledge and precious lessons, but you cannot live there. Likewise, the future does not actually exist; it is a construct of our own minds, and you cannot live there either.

So why is it that so many of us miss out on this precious present moment, where life *does* take place, by revisiting the past and ruminating over the things we cannot change, or by imagining the future, often in exactly the way we do not want it to occur.

In essence, the latter is the definition of anxiety; taking your powerful mind out to the future and imagining life playing out exactly as you do not want it to. With mindful awareness, we can recognise when we are running these old unhelpful patterns, and purposefully bring our attention back to the present moment, without judgement.

By using our breath to step out of stress mode, as described later in this handbook, we can change our internal chemistry, and ground ourselves in the here and now.

THE POWER OF MINDFULNESS

What research is saying and how it can help you!

MINDFULNESS INCREASES:

- cognition: processing of knowledge, understanding, attention, focus and clarity of thought.
- grey matter in the brain in the areas responsible for learning, memory and cardiorespiratory function
- cardiovascular health; heart and blood vessels
- gastrointestinal health; digestion
- reproductive health: fertility
- immune function; immunity
- general health; well-being
- circulating endorphins; happiness hormones

- empathy and compassion
- feelings of calm
- resilience
- emotional regulation
- mood
- empathy
- confidence
- self-esteem & self-awareness
- ability to cope
- social skills
- sleep
- job performance and satisfaction

MINDFULNESS REDUCES:

- anxiety
- rumination
- depression
- burnout
- wear and tear on body systems
- effects of stress
- inflammation
- autoimmune effects
- blood pressure
- heart rate
- circulating stress hormones
- negative effects on all body organs
- stress related blood glucose levels
- work-related stress

So, the practice of mindfulness sounds pretty good, I'm sure you will agree. I could go on and on and even write a whole book on its benefits, but I'm not going to reinvent the wheel here.

There are many excellent books on this subject if you are interested in reading further, and if this has ignited your interest, a quick Google search will provide you with an abundance of excellent quality, evidence-based research studies on this topic.

My aim here is to get your attention, I will now go on to condense much of what I have personally and professionally learned over many years of studying and practicing mindfulness into simplified and useable daily techniques. Incorporating these techniques into your life will enhance your experience in many positive ways.

Please refer to Part Two, **Helpful Techniques and Daily Practices**: *Mindful Practices.*

GRATITUDE

I often talk to my clients about the positive benefits of daily gratitude practice, and just as importantly, the positive outcomes from developing and maintaining a general 'attitude of gratitude' or 'gratitude mindset' during their day.

The positive benefits of practicing gratitude in your life are many.

Gratitude practices have been shown to be beneficial in creating positive emotional, social, and physical outcomes. In fact, there is now so much evidence-based research available, clearly illustrating the positive effects of embracing a daily practice of gratitude. This creates beneficial effects across all areas of our daily physical and emotional experiences.

Practising gratitude has been shown to produce the following outcomes:

Improvements in:

- long-term happiness and optimism
- immunity
- forgiveness and understanding
- interpersonal skills
- problem solving
- self-esteem
- contentment
- physical and emotional well-being
- resilience
- relationships
- restful sleep

Reductions in:

- self-centeredness
- greed
- anxiety
- depression
- suicidal thoughts

This is not an exhaustive list, but as you can see, practising daily gratitude has many of the same benefits as reducing stress and relieving the allostatic load on your bodily systems.

This is because when you practise gratitude, you are taking yourself out of stress by changing the focus of your powerful mind, thus creating a different chemical environment within your body.

I hope you are beginning to see the benefits of making simple, constructive, and repetitive changes to what you choose to focus your attention on. This will enable you to make significant and powerful changes in how you experience your life.

WHAT IS A GRATITUDE MINDSET?

Creating a 'gratitude mindset' involves embracing a daily focus of gratitude and appreciation, and placing that focus on the things we are grateful for.

I am aware some people will struggle with this concept, however the more you practise the easier it becomes. The key is to focus on the things often overlooked; the 'seemingly' little things. It is easy to say, 'I'm grateful for my holiday to Bali,' or '…for my new car'. However, it is important to focus daily on the smaller, yet still significant blessings; these will make a real difference to your 'gratitude mindset' and subsequent feelings of contentment and happiness.

You may ask, what do I have to be grateful for when everything in life seems to be falling apart? Perhaps your spouse has left you, or you have lost your job, or any number of adversities might consume your every waking moment, every waking thought, thereby creating a damaging and disastrous chemical cocktail in your body. You then very quickly begin to feel exactly the way you have just been thinking; – helpless, not good enough, anxious, or depressed – just to name a few, very common possibilities. If you continue to practise these ruminations unchecked, you will notice more and more of what is bad in your life.

It may be true that you can do nothing about what is happening around you, but what if you were to use your powerful potential to tune out from those damaging thoughts and ruminations, to tune into something else; things that have probably gone unnoticed amongst your pain and turmoil.

When we change our focus we can go on a search for the things in our life we are grateful for; the very same things we have often taken for granted; a warm bed, a roof over our head, food on the table, fresh hot and cold running water, a smile from a stranger, an act of kindness, electricity at your fingertips, a healthy family, the things we do have, and those things that are working for us. These are the things that, when focused on, will have a significant positive effect on our mindset.

If you have ever taken that holiday to Bali, Thailand or India – that you may have been so grateful for at the time – you will also have no doubt noticed that not everyone in this world has the blessings that we often take for granted; yet strangely, these people seem so happy. How can it be that we in western society, who materialistically have so much, also have the greatest reported levels of sadness, anxiety and depression in the world, whilst those with seemingly nothing in comparison to our affluent lifestyles, are blissfully happy? The answer may lie in their mindset: they are grateful. Grateful for the privilege to wait on you, to have a job, to earn a tiny wage to feed their family, to have a roof over their head. It is indeed a paradox that these people, who seemingly have so little in comparison to our western standards, are some of the happiest people you might ever encounter.

I'm sure many of you are now becoming aware that you have, in the past, unwittingly focused your powerful attention on the complete opposite of gratitude. Even on that wonderful holiday, you may have chosen to be overly-focused on the unpleasant coffee on the plane trip, the rude taxi driver from the airport, there not being enough soap in the bathroom, or even the fact you have a garden view room instead of a pool view room that would be so much better. Perhaps you chose to overly ruminate and focus on the things that seemingly went wrong, and the outcome of this is that you will have immediately begun to feel exactly the way you had been thinking: dissatisfied, annoyed, even angry. You may even have unintentionally gone on a search for other things that were not satisfactory and before you know it you will have sabotaged your holiday experience, and may choose to never go back to that destination again. The problem with your holiday, however, was never the destination, it was your own mindset.

This is not entirely your fault, you see human beings have a strong predisposition for negativity, we are wired that way. The reason for this genetic predisposition has its origins far back in human evolution. The purpose of the negative bias that we have inherited originally worked to keep us alive as a species when potential danger lurked around every corner.

In today's world, if this negative bias is left unchecked, it will predispose us to living a life of fear, anxiety, and depression, whilst at the same time embracing the opposite mindset to gratitude, one designed to look out for imminent danger. Therefore, we may feel compelled to focus on what is wrong, absent, or broken in our lives.

So, what can we do to counter this negative predisposition?

The answer is awareness. When we are aware of what we have been doing, often unknowingly, by running habits and patterns that do not serve us, we have the opportunity to begin the process of change.

At this point we are once again reminded of the power and potential of our focus of attention, which will be discussed further in other sections of this handbook.

Please refer to Part Two, **Helpful techniques and Daily Practices:** *Daily Gratitude Practices* for techniques you can implement each day.

MEDITATION

WHAT IS IT?

Meditation is an awareness practice, utilising specific techniques designed to allow us to focus on one thing, such as a thought, an object, a feeling, or an activity, with the aim to create clarity and calm.

WHY MEDITATE?

In my book 'Sarah's Story, life after IVF,' a Buddhist monk explains to my protagonist Sarah, that The Buddha once described the mind to be like a drunken monkey, wildly flinging itself from tree to tree whilst endlessly chattering.

In *The Power of Thoughts* Section of this HandBook I will talk about the massive power and potential of your thoughts to create change in your body. Meditation helps us to manage our thoughts, and in doing so we can find inner peace.

The aim of meditation, therefore, is to tame the mind, and in so doing, to create clarity, calm and physical wellbeing in the body.

The health benefits of meditation are many and include:

- reduced stress levels
- reduced physical muscular aches and pains, irritable bowel and fibromyalgia
- physical changes to the brain, including an increase in the brain's memory, cognition, and clarity
- reduction in the size of the brain's stress centre
- less depression and anxiety
- less reactivity
- improved attention
- increased compassion
- better sleep.

This list is not exhaustive, and as you progress through this handbook you may realise that the benefits of meditation are very similar to the listed benefits of stepping out of stress mode. This is because meditation is a very effective technique to help you do just that.

Whilst I will not ask or expect you to go and sit in a corner and meditate for hours on end, I will ask you to entertain the idea that there could be a meditation practice that will work for you.

TYPES OF MEDITATION

- mantra: the repetition of meaningful words or statements
- mindful: noticing what is happening in the present moment using all of your senses: sounds / sensations / feelings / smells / noises / tastes / sight if eyes are open
- focused:
- candle meditation
- loving-kindness
- gratitude
- care and compassion
- breath
- meditation guided by an experienced meditation practitioner
- sound meditation
- theta wave meditation
- sounds of nature
- singing bowls
- moving: Tai Chi / dance / whirling dervishes / mindful walking
- spiritual
- prayer
- seeking a deeper connection
- Buddhist:
- Samatha: Calming meditation leading to deeper connection
- Vipassana: Insight meditation
- transcendental: the mantra is specific to the individual and becomes a vehicle for transcending
- progressive muscle relaxation
- heart coherence meditation: bringing the heart and brain into a coherent state

There are many different types of meditation practices, ranging in duration from a few minutes to a few hours, so it's easy for you to find one that works for you.

Again, I will say that I am not here to reinvent the wheel, however I do want to stimulate your curiosity. There are plenty of very good meditation apps or courses you can attend to learn the various types of meditation, should you choose to do so. There are also many wonderful books written on the subject.

In this handbook I have focused on the simple practices that you can easily incorporate into a busy lifestyle, that will allow you to gain maximum benefit. I have also added the links to my **Danielle Aitken Clinical Hypnotherapist** *YouTube Channel* where you can access some of my basic guided techniques. So I encourage you to get curious here and explore what is available and what works best for you personally.

～

Please refer to Part Two, **Helpful Techniques and Daily Practices:** *Daily Meditation Practices*

LET'S TALK ABOUT THE HUMBLE BREATH

THE PHYSIOLOGY OF THE BREATH AND WHY IT IS IMPORTANT

Our inhalation, or 'in breath' connects us to our **sympathetic nervous system (SNS)**. This is the system responsible for rapid and involuntary responses to stressful situations. It is often called 'fight-flight mode', as previously mentioned in this handbook. Activation of the SNS results in stress hormones and chemicals being instantly released into the body's circulatory system. This release immediately increases alertness, pupil dilatation, heart rate, respiration, blood pressure, blood glucose, and even clotting factors; leading to thicker stickier blood that is ready to clot if we are injured. As this occurs, the body's resources are simultaneously shunted away from the non-essential bodily processes and functions that are not required to keep us alive in that specific moment: processes such as digestion, cognition, fertility, and immunity, amongst others. All available resources are therefore directed in an instant toward the extremities, preparing us to either fight or flee.

This is a wonderful and much needed physical response that human beings really want to instantly activate, if for example, we inadvertently walk in front of a speeding car. However, we are not supposed to live in stress mode. To do so creates the previously mentioned allostatic load on our body organs and systems that is damaging over time.

It is interesting to note that human beings, are the only species that can activate fight-flight mode inappropriately, using our thoughts alone, in the absence of any real threat.

Think about that for a moment.
If we are activating stress mode when we worry about a pending deadline: the presentation we need to do, the email we haven't sent, the fight we just had with a friend or family member, we are actually predisposing ourselves to have poor immune function, infertility, gastrointestinal dysfunction, autoimmune conditions, anxiety and even reduced cognition and/or dementia.

That is certainly food for thought!

Now for the good news. The exhalation, or out breath, on the other hand, connects us to our **parasympathetic nervous system (PNS).** Sometimes referred to as 'rest and digest mode', or 'relaxation response', a term coined by Herbert Benson, cardiologist and founder of Harvard's Mind/Body Medical institute, after his early work studying meditation in the 1960s and 1970s.

When we connect to PNS, our heart rate, respiration and blood pressure are all reduced. PNS is responsible for control of bodily functions when we are at rest. Such functions include stimulating digestion, metabolism, clarity of thought, and relaxation of smooth muscle.

I would like you to take a moment to think about this, and how your body already knows exactly what to do, in either situation. Your natural bodily responses happen with or without your conscious awareness. When you get a fright you will often take a quick inhalation, or even hold your breath in for a few seconds as your body springs into action, activating your SNS. Likewise, when you have had a big day and finally get to relax, you will probably take a long slow exhalation in the form of a sigh of relief, which instantly activates your PNS rest and digest mode.

SNS and PNS are part of the **autonomic nervous system** (ANS) that regulates involuntary processes in the body. However, **there is one process in the body which functions both involuntarily AND voluntarily! That function is the breath**. What this means for you is that you can use what we have just learned to communicate directly with the body in the language it understands. You can therefore consciously hijack the PNS's natural responses, and in doing so you can effectively and intentionally step out of stress or fight-flight mode at will.

WHY PRACTISE BREATH TECHNIQUES?

Daily practice of breath techniques trains the body to quickly respond to the breath at will, enabling you to rapidly bring calm into difficult and stressful situations.

BREATH TECHNIQUES CAN:

- help to reduce the sometimes paralysing symptoms of anxiety and even depression, by bringing you back into the present moment, where those things you are worrying about are not occurring.
- help reduce insomnia, by taking the focus away from night-time ruminations.
- help to reduce elevated blood pressure and other stress related health concerns.
- help interrupt old self-defeating patterns of thinking and feeling by providing a pattern interrupt, which, when practised often enough, can lead to a neurological rewiring as you begin to re-wire your brain for a calmer and more satisfying response.

- lead to more clarity of thought, thus you can be more productive at work and at home.
- reduce stress and help to boost your immune system.

There are so many other reasons to use breath-work as a part of your self-care practices, but the main ones really should be:

- **IT WORKS**
- **IT'S EASY**
- **IT'S AVAILABLE.**

Your breath is with you 24/7, and better than that, you can immediately connect to the relaxation benefits of a single breath, and nobody need ever know you are doing it.

THE RATIO TO REMEMBER: 1:2

Now we understand the function of the SNS and the PNS, we can hijack the body's natural mechanism of relaxation by taking a longer, slower exhalation, such that the out breath is twice as long as the in breath. This effectively sends a clear message to our body that we are safe. The body, therefore, immediately steps out of stress mode and into relaxation mode.

THERE ARE COUNTLESS BREATH TECHNIQUES

Q: **Which is the best one for you?**

A: *Only you will know.*

EXPERIMENT WITH VARIOUS BREATH TECHNIQUES AND FIND ONE THAT:

- feels comfortable
- is easy for you to use
- works well to relax your mind and body.

REMEMBER:
Depending on the length of your breath, on average four to six breaths will take ONLY one minute of your day.

I'm sure you can find one minute in your busy day.

ALSO

One minute, several times a day, will make an enormous difference to your overall emotional and physical well-being; effectively punctuating your day with a 'physiological stress-release valve' enabling you to reduce the cumulative level and effects of life's daily stressors.

For specific breath exercises please refer to Part Two, **Helpful Techniques and Daily Practices**: *Breath Techniques and Practices*

CONSCIOUS AND SUBCONSCIOUS AWARENESS

THE CONSCIOUS MIND

Your conscious mind is the part of your mind that deals with:

- logic
- judgement
- planning
- evaluation
- thinking
- learning.

Basically, it is the part of your mind that makes sense of things.

**According to cognitive neuroscientists, it is responsible for ONLY between 5-7% of our cognitive activity!
It is therefore understandable that the conscious mind is known to have a limited capacity to retain information at any given moment in time.**

If you have ever attempted one of those memory games in which a list of objects is read to you, and you must recall it back, you will probably have an understanding of what this statement means.

The information is stored in the subconscious mind; you will recognise the word as soon as it is told to you, and berate yourself for not remembering it, but most people just don't have the conscious capacity to store the number of items on the list for immediate recall.

Conservatively it is thought that the average person's conscious mind can only retain between 4-7 pieces of information at one time, which is a little scary when you think about it!

THE SUBCONSCIOUS MIND

Some may call this the 'unconscious' mind, but due to my nursing background, I personally prefer to call it subconscious, as we are certainly not unconscious, at least in the medical interpretation of the word, when we access this part of the mind.

The subconscious mind is a powerhouse at our individual disposal; that part of the mind that is happy to respond immediately – chemically and physically – to every thought we have. It is always waiting for instructions. If you have read the earlier part of this handbook, this may be starting to sound somewhat familiar.

YOUR SUBCONSCIOUS MIND:

- is not logical
- does not judge
- accepts information without evaluation
- stores all memories
- cannot differentiate between reality or imagination
- stores emotional responses
- runs the functioning of the body
- runs habits / good or bad
- is the mind of mastery.

Basically, our subconscious mind is responsible for 93-95% of all brain activity: every function or action we take that we are not consciously aware of, anything we do whilst on auto pilot is being run by the subconscious mind, including all things we have mastered, like driving a car.

If you recall the process of learning to drive, you may remember that you were very conscious of every step. Now you probably don't give it a second thought, because you have mastered driving, and your subconscious mind can drive better than the conscious mind ever could.

You may well ask, why is it important for you to know this?

It is important because we can use the mighty potential of the subconscious mind to create our desired outcomes, by focusing our attention on what we want, and imagining we have already achieved it. We can create change faster and more effectively with the subconscious mind than would ever be possible with the conscious mind.

'How?' I hear you ask. Great question!

Read on………

THE POWER OF THOUGHT

BELIEFS: WHAT ARE THEY AND WHY ARE THEY IMPORTANT?

A belief is something that you accept to be true, with or without supporting evidence.

Beliefs consist of thoughts that form our personal narrative, or our story. The *'I'm useless'* story, the *'I can't do it'* story or the *'I'll never amount to anything'* story, for example. If these are our beliefs, we will often notice evidence in our daily experiences that validates and strengthens these beliefs, in exclusion of all the evidence that contradicts them. These stories therefore contribute to the creation of our personal reality, however what is reality really?

Have you ever noticed that two people who have experienced the exact same situation will later have very different recollections of the event? One person may believe that last summer was the hottest we have had for years, while another person will absolutely believe it was the coldest, or wettest. This is because we cannot consciously take in all available information, so we filter, distort and generalise bits of information to suit our personal narrative. In other words. what we focus on we notice more of, often disproportionately.

I hope you are beginning to see that what we 'believe' is pivotal.

A QUOTE TO REMEMBER

*Henry Ford once rightly said:
'Whether you think you can, or you think you can't,
You're right!'*

YOU ARE WHAT YOU THINK: SELF-FULFILLING PROPHECIES

Scientific research has found that whenever we have a thought, our bodies immediately respond with a cascade of chemicals and hormones that are directly related to that thought. Therefore, if you wake up in the morning and you go in search of that ache or pain, not only are you bringing it into awareness, whereby you will notice it more intensely, you are also inadvertently strengthening the neural pathway that is keeping it firing and wiring.

If you are thinking anxiety-provoking thoughts, your body will respond by showering your internal environment with stress chemicals that will almost instantly make you feel the way you were just thinking. Because you now feel anxious, you begin to think more anxious thoughts which leads to even more anxiety. As previously mentioned, human beings can create a full-blown panic attack with their thoughts alone. We are the only species that can inappropriately trigger this fight-flight response when there is no actual danger. Therefore, if you think anxious thoughts, you will feel anxious. If you think sad thoughts, you will feel sad, and conversely, if you think happy or empowering thoughts, you will feel happy or empowered.

This is the good news, because believe it or not, we *can* control our thoughts, when we know how.

YESTERDAY'S THOUGHTS RECREATE YESTERDAY'S PROBLEMS - TODAY

If you wake in the morning and immediately begin to think yesterday's thoughts, you are dragging yesterday's problems right back into the present moment.

In order to create change we need to choose to act, think or feel differently.

Instead, when you open your eyes ask yourself the question:

WHO DO I CHOOSE TO BE TODAY?

To become something else, we need to do something else: choose different thoughts, to choose different feelings and to choose different behaviours. In essence we have to become visionaries developing a clear knowing and understanding of where we are heading; to really know what the destination looks like and feels like.

This is essential if we are to achieve our goals.

I often say to my clients, If I were to ask you to get into your car now and without the use of your GPS, drive to Kununurra, an Australian town, and If you don't know in which direction to head – perhaps you don't know where Kununurra is, or what Kununurra looks like, or even how it feels to be in Kununurra – it is highly probable that you will never get there.

So, the things we need to consider are:

- What will my destination look like?
- What will my destination feel like?
- What will I need to focus on to lead me towards my destination?
- What is one thing I can do today that will lead me in the direction of my destination?

Remember,
If you take one small step in the direction of your goal, by doing one thing differently you will change your course and in doing so, create a different outcome.

CHANGE YOUR THOUGHTS, CHANGE YOUR FEELINGS, CHANGE YOUR OUTCOMES....HOW?

We have now established that our thoughts and beliefs are very important, so it is essential that we choose very carefully which thoughts we allow to take up occupancy in the very prime real estate of our minds.

If a belief is an acceptance that something exists or is true, and a belief can exist in the absence of any real proof, it is not surprising that many of our beliefs can be negative and can lead to low self-esteem, a lack of confidence, or feelings of inadequacy. Negative beliefs can often be based on false assumptions that are deeply embedded in the subconscious mind. They are pivotal to your outcomes, which means you must deal with any limiting beliefs you have been carrying with you like a millstone around your neck. Just like negative thoughts, the more you bring your negative beliefs and the many manifestations of them into conscious awareness, the better able you are to begin to challenge them and shift them.

Awareness is the key here; as soon as you are aware of anything, it gives you the opportunity to do something about it.

So, we now have established that your thoughts and your beliefs have a pivotal impact on your outcomes, but which thoughts are the most important would you think?

It's the ones you focus on, and the ones you believe to be true.

SELF-TALK: WHAT IS A NEGATIVE AUTOMATIC THOUGHT?

These are thoughts that are:

- automatic
- thoughts you have told yourself many times
- thoughts you believe on some level
- thoughts that are damaging in nature

- thoughts that contribute to the story you are believing about yourself, that form part of your internal narrative.

Automatic, negative thoughts, feelings or beliefs are something we all need to be aware of. This is the constant, often negative chatter in our own heads which leads us to subconscious beliefs and expectations about who we are and what we can, or can't, achieve. The more we run these old patterns of thinking and feeling, the more we strengthen the neural pathways that keep them running. Thus, it is important to be very aware of this chatter and to interrupt the pattern and replace it with a more productive thought and/or feeling.

Some of the negative self-chatter that I often hear clients saying, and more importantly believing, are statements such as those listed.

COMMON NEGATIVE AUTOMATIC THOUGHTS

- I'm useless.
- I'm not worthy.
- I don't deserve it.
- I'm stupid.
- I'm not good enough.
- Nobody will love me.
- I can't do it.
- I always fail.
- I can't change.
- I'm not safe.
- I'll never be able to achieve it.

- I should be better.
- Everyone else can do it.
- I don't fit in.
- It will always be this way.

You may notice that many of these self-limiting statements are connected to self-defeating words.

STATEMENTS, WORDS AND PHRASES TO BE AWARE OF:

Words such as those in the list below, can often act as a red flag or warning sign enabling you to identify the offending self-limiting narrative that you are currently running.

- **I should...**
- **I won't...**
- **I'll never...**
- **I always...**
- **I can't...**
- **I must...**
- **I have to...**
- **Everyone else** can/has/will...
- **No one else** feels this way.

Your thoughts are powerful. Becoming aware that you are using these words or phrases is an essential first step.

I find it is often good to reflect upon what you would say or think, if someone else said these things to you.

- Would you accept this?
- Would you believe it?
- Would you be offended?
- Would you be outraged?
- Would you get angry?

I mean really, how dare someone ever say to you; *'you're not good enough'*, or *'You'll fail for sure'*.

So why is it we often constantly tell ourselves the very things we would never accept others saying about us? More importantly, how can we change this self-destructive internal chatter?

Here is a quick 3-step technique to practise now:

- **STEP 1** : Become aware that you are having an unpleasant thought or feeling.
- **STEP 2** : Challenge the thought/feeling by creating separation between you and it. There are many ways to do this, but the most important question you can ask yourself is, '*Is this helpful?*'
- If the answer is no, go to Step 3
- **STEP 3**: Take a breath and return to present moment awareness.

You have 60-80,000 thoughts a day!
However, it is important to remember, **you always get to choose** which ones you focus your powerful attention on?

Please refer to Part Two, **Helpful Techniques and Daily Practices:** *Your Thoughts are Powerful* for a detailed description of *The Pattern Interrupt*.

YOUR SOLUTION STATE

WHAT IS IT?

- **Your *'solution state'*** is you imagining your life as though the problem that has been troubling you, and all its implications, has completely vanished, and no longer exists in your life.
- **Your *'solution state'*** needs to be imagined in the present moment, not in the future; rather, as though you have already achieved it.
- **Your *'solution state'*** needs to be as far away from the problem as possible, almost like flipping a coin or going 180 degrees in the opposite direction.

YOU WILL NEED TO *REALLY* KNOW

- What it will look like.
- What it will feel like.
- What are the emotions connected with this state?
- What are the tastes, smells, colours connected *(If any)*?
- What are you doing that has made the difference in your experience?
- What are you no longer doing that has made the difference?

Your **'solution state'** is another way of formulating your goal. The language used here becomes very important when you begin to understand how this works.

As discussed previously, your powerful subconscious mind cannot tell the difference between what is real and what is imagined. It will therefore respond to your thoughts as though they *are* real, even when they are not. Sitting in the problem state, you have become very skilled at applying this principal, just in the reverse. Thus it is paramount to choose your words and your thoughts wisely.

If anxiety has been your problem, then having no anxiety is ***not*** your solution. The moment you mention the word 'anxiety', even if you are saying I won't have it, your subconscious mind will delete the negative prefix and immediately respond to the word it knows so well – 'anxiety'. When this happens, powerful chemicals and hormones are instantly released into your bloodstream and surge through your body, and before you know it you are feeling the way you were just thinking, and the next unhelpful thought that you experience may be something akin to: 'This isn't working.' or 'I can't do this.' or 'I have anxiety, I can't change that'.

Instead, we need to imagine the complete opposite to the problem and describe it in positive language as shown below.

Your Current PROBLEM

Be very specific, **how, where, when** and **why** this is a problem for you.

For example:

- anxiety
- insomnia
- rumination
- I can't work
- Low self esteem
- I'm never good enough
- I can't get my message across
- I can't think clearly
- tension in my body
- tightness in the chest
- mental fog
- constant pain
- heavy feelings weighing me down
- everything feels unsafe
- darkness

Your GOAL or SOLUTION
This is you when the problem no longer exists

- calm
- sleeping well
- being productive
- proud of myself
- happy being me
- communicating well
- being heard
- relief
- comfortable in my skin
- clarity
- relaxed, comfortable body

- at peace
- like a weight has lifted
- feeling safe
- light and bright

∼

Please refer to Part Two, **Helpful Techniques and Daily Practices:** for more information on *Creating your 'solution state'*.

HEART-BRAIN COHERENCE

WHAT IS HEART-BRAIN COHERENCE?

The latest research from the HeartMath Institute is clearly showing that this is a powerful tool to create change.

As a certified *HeartMath Practitioner*, I have utilised this meditation with wonderful effect to heal my own body and to assist my clients in their own healing. The Heart-Brain Coherence meditation technique is simple, practical, and user-friendly; it accesses the intelligence of the heart, shifting its rhythms from incoherent – in times of stress – to coherence. This results in different neurological messages being sent to the brain. The technique is based on thirty years of research from the HeartMath institute established in 1991, that shows that connecting to the heart in a specific way, utilising positive emotions, creates beneficial chemical and physical changes in the body.

The evidence shows that negative emotions and stress create chaos in the body. Conversely, positive emotions, such as gratitude, care and compassion create coherence. When this happens, it has been shown to lead to a boost in immunity, an increase in creativity, mental clarity, problem solving and intuition. The healing chemistry that is released into the blood stream, due to the coherence of heart and brain, leads to beneficial effects that have been measured to last up to six hours in the body.

HOW IT WORKS:

A recent discovery has uncovered that the heart has its own system of neurons: brain cells called sensory neurites. This meditation allows for the neurons in the heart and the neurons in the brain to synchronise, creating a coherent rhythm between these organs which establishes a new baseline leading to sustained improvements in health over time.

I cannot recommend this meditation highly enough. I practise it every day. It is simple and effective and has been pivotal in my own healing journey.

Please refer to Part Two, **Helpful Techniques and Daily Practices:** *Heart Coherent Breathing Technique.*

If you want to know more about this meditation, please refer to
The HeartMath Institute at
https://www.heartmath.org

Also Please refer to my YouTube Channel:
**Danielle Aitken Clinical Hypnotherapy
Heart Coherence Meditation**

PART TWO

**HELPFUL TECHNIQUES
AND
DAILY PRACTICES**

HELPFUL TECHNIQUES AND DAILY PRACTICES

I invite you to try a variety of these techniques.

The goal here is to learn and become comfortable with a variety of techniques that work best for you, so that you may utilise them when you need them most; anywhere, anytime, in order to step out of stress or anxiety at will.

Please go to my YouTube Channel.
'Danielle Aitken Clinical Hypnotherapist'
to guide you through many of these techniques if you think this will be beneficial.

Danielle

BREATH TECHNIQUES AND PRACTICES

The breath is a wonderful tool you can utilise to efficiently take you out of stress mode at will.
The more you practise these breath techniques when you are *not* stressed, the more you will be able to draw on the positive benefits of them, quickly and effectively, when needed.

There are many different breath techniques, these are just a few. I invite you to explore these and other techniques until you find those that feel right for you.

4:7:8 BREATH:

This technique is based on an ancient yogic breath technique, made popular more recently by Dr Andrew Weil MD.

STEPS

- Empty the lungs completely; through the mouth. You may wish to make an audible whooshing sound as you exhale.
- Breathe in silently/gently through the nose to the count of 4.
- Hold the breath to the count of 7.
- Breathe out long and slowly through the mouth, *making a whooshing sound,* to the count of 8.
- Relax the shoulders and any muscular tightness during the long slow exhalation.
- Repeat this breath cycle of inhalation, hold and exhalation **four times** only.

After two to four weeks of practice and feeling comfortable with this technique using four breath cycles, you can increase to eight breath cycles. **Eight breath cycles** is the **maximum** you should do for this particular technique.

Continued practice of 4:7:8 breath technique has shown to create improvements in clients experiencing problematic anxiety and depression.

BREATHE IN, BREATHE OUT, RELAX

I find this technique useful for those of us who need a little reminder to relax and let go of muscular tension. It's as though the word relax at the end of the exhalation gives you permission to do just that. This is a favourite of mine.

STEPS

- Breathe in for a comfortable, but full breath.
- Breathe out comfortably for the same length of time.
- Extend the exhalation making it slightly longer as you quietly say the word RELAX to yourself, a reminder to drop your shoulders and release any remaining muscular tension you have been holding in your body.
- Repeat for one to two minutes.
- Get curious about how you feel in your body and mind as you allow calm and relaxation to deepen.

4: 8 BREATH

This is a simple two step technique. As for all breath techniques, you will notice the period of the exhalation is twice as long as the inhalation. Remember we are connecting to the parasympathetic nervous system here. The PNS is stimulated by the exhalation which triggers our 'relaxation' mode.

STEPS

- Breathe in for the count of 4: PAUSE.
- Breathe out for the count of 8, fully emptying the lungs: PAUSE.
- Relax into the exhalation by dropping your shoulders and releasing any other muscular tension held in the body.
- Repeat for one to two minutes.

4:4:8 BREATH

This is a good one for those who find the 'seven hold', in the 4:7:8 breath a little difficult. For all breath techniques, it is essential that they are comfortable. The benefit of the technique is lost if it is causing you difficulty and you cannot relax fully.

STEPS

- Breathe in to the count of 4
- Hold to the count of 4 .
- Breathe out to the count of 8 .
- Relax deeply into each exhalation.
- Repeat this breath cycle for several minutes.

MINDFUL BREATH

Mindfulness is about allowing your focus to be in the present moment. Therefore, when mindfully breathing you are focusing on the here and now, becoming curious about what you can observe and feel, as the experience of the breath is allowed to gently unfold, moment by moment.

STEPS

- Sit quietly where you will not be disturbed.
- Allow the breath to flow without trying to alter it.
- Gently breathe in through the nose.
- Notice where the inhalation touches the skin.
- Be aware of the temperature of the air on the inhalation.
- Gently breathe out through the nose.
- Notice where the exhalation touches the skin.
- Be aware the temperature of the air on the exhalation.
- Gently allow the exhalation to lengthen and relax right into the out breath, surrendering completely to the relaxation.
- Get curious about the gentle rise and fall of your chest.
- Notice without judgement where you feel the breath in your body: the nostrils / chest / abdomen.
- Again, notice the gentle ebb and flow of the breath in these areas.
- Notice your immediate environment.
- Become curious about what you can see, feel and hear.

Continue for two to five minutes, bringing your awareness to the present moment, breath by breath.

COUNTING THE BREATH

In this technique, as you relax deeply into each exhalation, allow yourself to completely surrender to the experience of focusing your full attention on the count of your breath.

STEPS

- Sit comfortably and close your eyes.
- Focus your attention on your breath, allowing it to be slightly slower and deeper than usual.
- Breathe in slowly to the count of 1.
- Breathe out slowly relaxing deeply into the exhalation.
- Breathe in slowly to the count of 2.
- Breathe out slowly, continuing to relax deeply into the exhalation throughout this entire exercise.
- Breathe in slowly to the count of 3.

Continue breathing like this, up to the count of 10, then begin to count down with each breath, back to the count of 1 as follows:

- Breathe in slowly to the count of 10.
- Breathe out slowly relaxing into the exhalation.
- Breathe in slowly to the count of 9…and so on, all the way back to 1.

BOX BREATHING

With each inhalation, exhalation and hold of this exercise, imagine in your mind that you are making your way methodically around the inside of a box.

STEPS

- Close your eyes and imagine a square box.
- Breathe in slowly to the count of 4.
- Hold to the count of 4.
- Breathe out slowly to the count of 4.
- Hold to the count of 4.

I find it helpful to imagine moving up with the inhalation, crossing from side to side with the hold, and dropping down with the release on exhalation.

Have fun with this one.

HEART FOCUSED BREATH

With this breath we are placing the attention on your heart. You may find it helpful to gently touch your chest, in the area of your heart, because our focus will always be drawn to the area of the touch.

STEPS

- Allow your focus to drop from your busy mind to your feeling heart in the area of the middle of your chest.
- You may choose to place a hand over this area.
- Imagine that it is possible for you to breathe in and out of this heart focused place beneath the hand.
- Allow the breath to be slightly deeper and slower than usual.
- Breathe in to the count of 5.
- Breathe out to the count of 6.
- Be aware of the gentle rise and fall of your hand as the breath flows in and out.
- Continue this breath for two to three minutes maintaining a heart focus.

As you can see from these few examples, there are so many breath techniques you can practise. None are better than others, but some will work better for you.

I advise you to find one or two that feel comfortable and are easy for you to fit into your schedule. Practise them a few minutes each day. The benefit of practicing these techniques when you are feeling calm, is that you will be able to anchor a calm state to the exhalation that is then able to be utilised at other times of stress during your busy day.

Remember Hebb's Rule?

Practice will enable you to rewire your brain for more positivity and calm, which will be available to you when you really need it most.

PRACTICES TO ENHANCE NEUROPLASTICITY

AWARENESS IS THE KEY

There are many essentials to creating a healthy mind and enhancing neuroplasticity such as:

- maintaining a healthy diet
- having adequate rest
- getting adequate deep sleep
- learning a new language
- learning to play an instrument
- doing something differently by changing your routine
- challenging yourself to learn a new activity
- doing crosswords, word-searches or sudoku
- learning a new card game
- playing neuroplasticity-strengthening computer games
- exercising daily
- embracing mindfulness
- using breath techniques

- learning moving meditation; Tai Chi or Qigong
- establishing a meditation practice
- embracing a daily gratitude practice
- focusing on what is working
- focusing on the emotions of care and compassion
- interrupting your negative self-talk
- challenging limiting thoughts
- visualising your solution: see it, feel it, imagine it
- embracing the positive emotions of your solution state
- repetition, repetition, **REPETITION!**

So it is clear from this list that learning something new, or doing something differently are important factors in enhancing neuro-plasticity, however there is another very important factor, and that is **repetition**.

It is imperative to remember here that if repetition created your problem, repetition can create your solution, in fact it is essential!

Here we are going to focus on activities and techniques that impact your neurology and lead to your ability to change old habits and patterns that have created the problems you have been experiencing.

Old patterns and habits have become hard-wired in your brain by repetition, to the point where they often seem to be out of your control.

These techniques will give you back your control. Every time you interrupt one of those old patterns you weaken the neural pathway that has kept it wired.

Every time you change the focus to something else, be it a mindful breath or your solution state, you strengthen the neural pathway that runs the new, more empowering thought, feeling or behaviour, and this is how we create change.

> Awareness AND repetition are the keys to unlock the changes you desire. I know I have said that before, however I'm just checking that you are paying attention. ☺

Becoming aware of your triggers is essential in this process of creating change. Your triggers may be emotional, physical or situational.

As mentioned previously, when you become aware of anything, be it repetitive thoughts, feelings or behaviours, it effectively puts you in the driver's seat, whereby you get to decide what to do next.

> **'How do I become more aware,' I hear you ask?**

> There are many ways, journaling is one of them, mindfulness is another.

JOURNALING

Journaling has been associated with many health benefits, including reduced stress and increased wellbeing. Studies have also shown journaling is linked to increased daily productivity.

Some of you may choose to get a small notebook and carry it with you, while others may prefer to do this activity on your electronic devices, such as a mobile phone, either is fine.

It is important to journal at the time of experiencing the habit, thought, or feeling.

STEPS

- Choose to journal **when, where** and **how often** the symptoms present themselves, and your habit is triggered.
- Journaling creates knowledge as it brings the subconscious habits and patterns into conscious awareness.
- Journaling shines a light on the negative patterns illuminating them as they become more conscious.
- Journaling is a tangible way to monitor your progress, as it allows you to become more aware of the occurrence, frequency and duration of the presenting issue, and also allows you to notice the improvements over time.
- Journaling also enables you to be aware of the effectiveness of specific interventions on the occurrence, duration and frequency of the presenting issue/symptoms.

What to notice

- What are you doing at the time?
- Is anyone else present?
- What time does it happen?
- Can you identify a trigger?
- Can you identify any patterns?
- Note the duration of the symptom / habit.
- Note the severity of the symptom / habit on a scale of 1 to 10.

- How compelled did you feel to have to complete the habit or focus on the symptom on a scale of 1-10?

As you become more adept at tuning into the things that previously went unnoticed, you will then get to choose which of these repetitive thoughts, feelings, emotions, or behaviours to hold onto and which ones to let go of.

It is paramount to recognise here that the patterns and habits you choose to repeat are wiring your brain for more of the same.

So, how do we stop repeating the patterns and habits that no longer serve us?

Once we become aware of our self-defeating habits and patterns, we are able to begin the process of interrupting these redundant and damaging programs, and as we do, we begin rewiring the brain for a different response.

INTERRUPTING OLD PATTERNS

Remember and practise the formula:

- **Step 1:** I'm aware.
- **Step 2:** Is this helpful?
- **Step 3:** Change the focus and take a breath.

When you repeatedly change your focus; over and over again, the repetitive thoughts, feelings and behaviours you have previously been subjected to will diminish or even cease to return over time as your brain is rewired to respond in a different way.

It is important to remember, however, if one of those old thoughts does pop into your mind, or perhaps you find yourself feeling an old uncomfortable feeling, **do not judge it.** When we judge the thought or feeling we are giving it attention and inadvertently strengthening it. Neurologically, the more traffic we give the neural pathway that runs the repetitive thought, feeling or behaviour, the more likely it is to fire again. Don't forget Hebb's Rule: *Neurons that fire together wire together.*

Instead notice without judgement and proceed with step two and three of our pattern interrupt technique.

For more information on the pattern interrupt technique please refer to *Challenging Unhelpful Thoughts* in this part of the handbook.

LINKING

Linking is a process of connecting one well-established routine that you already practise every day to a new routine or habit that you want to establish. The rationale behind this is the existing strongly wired habit, will act as a trigger for you to run your new routine.

So, what is it you do many times a day?

- Make a cup of tea or coffee.
- Pick up your phone.
- Go to the bathroom.
- Wash your hands and look in the mirror.

- If every time you see yourself in the mirror you take thirty seconds to really immerse yourself in your solution state, and for that moment really believe you have achieved it, you will be firing and wiring your new response.
- If every time you put the kettle on you decide to take four long slow deliberate breaths, you will be reducing your stress levels and wiring the brain for more calm.
- If every time you wake up in the morning you think of five things you are grateful for, you will be establishing and hardwiring an attitude of gratitude.
- If every time you finish work you put on your walking shoes and go for a walk, you will be establishing an exercise routine.

STEPS

- Think about something that you already do often in your day; this could be brushing your teeth, making a cup of coffee, looking in the bathroom mirror, finishing work, or dropping the children at school.
- Choose an appropriate new behaviour to link to your established habit.
- Allow your established habit/routine to be the trigger to run your new habit (as above).
- It is important to be specific and detailed here.

SCHEDULING

Be specific, detailed and kind to yourself.

When you schedule in the exercise you want to achieve, or the study you wish to complete, or even the meditation practice you want to establish it is important to schedule it into your day at a time and place that it will actually be possible.

If you say, 'I want to exercise three times a week' and you haven't scheduled specific times, it may well get to Friday and you will have done nothing to achieve your goal.

Instead of this, if you schedule your activity for 9:30 on a Tuesday morning directly after school drop-off, or 5 o'clock on a Thursday immediately after work, you will be far more likely to achieve your goal:

Why ?

Because you have planned it at a time that works for you. You have made an appointment with yourself, and you have the expectation that this is the time you will complete that task.

This is no different to going to work or attending an appointment at the doctor's. These things happen because you have scheduled them into your life, so when 9:30 on a Tuesday morning, or 5pm on a Thursday evening arrives you know this is the time you have allocated to exercise.

I often say to my friends and family, if it isn't in my diary, it's just not going to happen, and this is true for most of us even though we may not be aware.

I therefore ask my clients who have a stressful job or a busy home life, who may perceive *'there is no time to practise self-care'*, to find a space in their busy day to schedule their desired activity in. Even four purposeful breaths, which will take approximately one minute, when practised several times a day, will make an extraordinary difference to your experience over time.

Establishing your new habits really can be as simple as, when I open my eyes in the morning, I will take four, slow, deep grounding breaths, or when I wake in the morning, I will close my eyes and I will focus on what I am grateful for, or I will go in search of what is working in my life or focus my attention on my intention for the day. Each time you complete your new activity, you will be firing and wiring your new program, strengthening the neural pathway that runs it and establishing it as your new habit.

STEPS

- Think about what you want to achieve. For example; establishing new routines for; exercise, study, meditation or a gratitude practice.
- Review your current schedule.
- Notice when it **is possible** to fit in your desired activity.
- It is important to consider your responsibilities, relationships and your physical surroundings here.
- Choose a time that **can** work for you.
- Schedule your activity: **the day, date, time** in a diary or planner so when that time arrives you know this is the time you have chosen to do the task.
- Let others know you are not available at this time.
- Turn off distractions.
- Make time for yourself.

MINDFUL PRACTICES

CONNECTING TO THE BREATH

Being mindful often involves connecting to the breath to be here and now, grounded in the moment-by-moment experiences of the body.

During breath-work mindful exercises, you allow the focus of attention to be fully on the breath. Noticing the gentle ebb and flow of the inhalation and exhalation and where and how you experience it, utilising all your senses.

Please refer to *Breath Techniques and Practices* for specific breath exercises.

MINDFUL BODY SCAN PRACTICE

As with many of these practices, with the body scan we utilise the breath to assist in relaxing the physical body.

STEPS:

- Ensure you are in a safe place where you will not be disturbed.
- Sit or lay down.
- Allow your eyes to close.
- Focus your attention on your breath.
- Allow the exhalation to be slightly longer than the inhalation and intentionally drop your shoulders as you exhale.
- Allow any muscular tightness held in the body to begin to melt away with every long, slow, exhalation.
- Working down through your entire body, muscle group by muscle group, begin at your forehead, and with each exhalation release and loosen the muscles of your face, jaw, neck, shoulders, arms, hands, fingers, upper back, lower back, chest, abdomen, thighs, calves, ankles and feet right down to your toes.
- At the completion of this practice, scan your body for any remaining muscular tightness and consciously allow it to be released with the next exhalation.
- Return your focus of attention to the relaxation you are creating in your body, breath by breath, muscle by muscle. Any thoughts that interrupt this practice can be noticed without judgement and allowed to drift away.

MINDFUL EATING

**Many of us are in the habit of eating mindlessly, often placing our hand in a bag of food only to find it empty, and we can't even remember eating it.
Sound familiar?**

When we eat mindfully, however, we do so with complete awareness and with full attention, as we slow down the entire process of eating, savouring each mouthful.

STEPS

- Allow time to fully appreciate what you are eating.
- Think about your food and give it your full attention.
- Turn off or remove distractions such as TV or phones.
- Enjoy the experience of eating.
- Chew smaller than usual portions ten to twenty times.
- Put your knife and fork down between mouthfuls as you focus on what is in your mouth.
- Using all your senses, notice the taste, texture, smell, colour and even the temperature of the food.
- Think about the nutrients the food brings to your body.
- Notice how the taste changes in a single mouthful.
- Notice how long it takes to dissolve the food in your mouth.
- Get curious as to how long you can chew a single mouthful.
- Notice the feeling of satisfaction you get from really appreciating small quantities of food.
- **It may be of interest to note that, when we embrace the practice of mindful eating, we often lose weight!**

MINDFUL DRINKING

Have you ever really watched a wine taster, and how they appreciate every aspect of the wine they are drinking? It can take many minutes before they even get the glass to their lips to take the smallest sip.

STEPS

- Hold the drink in your hands.
- Notice the temperature.
- Notice how you respond to the temperature.
- Is it warm and comforting or cool and chilled?
- How does the drink look? Notice the colour, the clarity.
- Now smell the aroma, notice how that makes you feel.
- Now you have used your senses to explore the temperature, colour, clarity and aroma, bring it to your lips and take the smallest sip.
- Savour the taste.
- Notice if the taste changes on the palate.
- Notice how you feel.
- Do you feel satisfied?

How much more enjoyment has this exploration given you?

MINDFUL VIEWING

If you are soothed by visual scenes around you, the colours and subtle hues of nature, I invite you to give this exercise a try.

You may like to do this by a window with a view, but for full effect research tells us that stepping into nature and fully immersing yourself in the experience is wonderfully good for our mental health; thus I would recommend going out into nature whenever you can. Get curious about the world around you, take at least five minutes to do this as you allow yourself to be fully present in this activity.

STEPS

- Take yourself to your place of viewing.
- As with all mindful practices, take a breath, relax your shoulders with the exhalation, and fully ground yourself in the present moment.
- Begin by noticing something in your line of vision. It might be a leaf of a tree or a blade of grass.
- Take time to get curious about it.
- Look at the colour variations, how it moves in the breeze, and whether there is other life around it: ants, bees, butterflies or birds.
- Notice the microcosm that exists as you explore with interest and discover what has previously gone unnoticed.
- Once you have fully explored one aspect, change your focus and discover something else.

I remember when I first did this, I became fascinated with the world of nature that existed in a tiny segment of my garden: how the dewdrops on the grass reflected the sun and created a sparkling light show; how the leaves and blades of grass moved gently in the breeze creating a previously unnoticed dance; and how ants and tiny insects existed in a micro-world of their own, for the most part unobserved by me. The experience allowed me to ground myself in the present moment of the here and now, creating a feeling of calm and a sense of coming home.

MINDFUL LISTENING

Now this is one that is so important for all our relationships.

It is very easy to tell when someone really isn't paying attention to what you are saying, and for me, this doesn't feel very good at all, especially if I am saying something that is important to me.

I'm sure you may agree, not being heard can lead to feelings of frustration and stress as we often can be left feeling undervalued or disrespected. This, however, is something we can all be guilty of in this busy world in which we live.

How often have you found yourself in conversation with someone, and you suddenly realise your mind has been somewhere else and you were not really listening. After such times, your partner may say in an accusing tone 'I told you that!,' but you swear that it's the first you have heard of it! Both of you may well be correct. Your partner may have told you, yet you really do not know anything about it, because you were somewhere else at the time. This can be the source of so many disagreements with family, friends or work colleagues, however it can so easily be corrected by implementing mindful listening practices.

STEPS

- Stop what you are doing.
- Put down devices and turn off other distractions.
- Face the person you are speaking to.
- Look them in the eyes.

- Give them your full attention.
- Allow them to speak without interruption.
- Really listen to what they are saying.
- Think about their message.
- Notice their tone and pace.
- Really hear what they are saying.
- Get curious about their message.
- Ensure you understand what they are saying by asking clarifying questions when it is your turn to speak.
- Be 100% present.

It is so validating to feel that you have been heard and understood.

Some of my clients will use a *'talking stick'* that gets passed from person to person for this activity. It's a fun way to be present and a reminder that the person with the stick is the one who can speak uninterrupted.

UTILISING ALL YOUR SENSES TO BE FULLY PRESENT IN NATURE

There have been countless studies that are indicating that participating in mindful activities whilst being in nature can lead to a reduction of depression and anxiety. It has also been shown to have a beneficial effect on not only our mental health, but also our physical well-being leading to a reduction of stress related disorders.

This is a simple activity that can really make you feel great. You don't need to go for a 10 km hike or bush walk, although both are wonderful options. This can be as simple as stepping outside of your front or back door. The aim of this exercise is to use all of your senses and get really curious about what you can discover.

STEPS

- Find yourself a space where you can be in the great outdoors away from distractions for five to ten minutes.
- Take a mindful breath.
- Relax into the exhalation as you drop your shoulders.
- As you continue to breathe, notice the temperature of the air. It will feel different on the inhalation and exhalation.
- Explore where it touches your skin.
- Continue to drop your shoulders on the exhalation, this sends a message to your body that you are safe, allowing you to be fully present.
- At this point you may wish to close your eyes. Closing the eyes can allow the other senses to be more acute.
- Take a moment to feel grounded in this place.
- Explore with your sense of smell.
- See if you can discover five things you can smell: the scents of nature – flowers, mown grass, perfume, cooking smells
- Now get curious about what you can hear:
- the sound of the wind
- birds: perhaps see if you can identify the different bird calls
- the ocean
- running water
- children playing
- a lawn mower or a car engine

- see how many things you can hear.
- Notice any bodily sensations:
- the feel of the wind or the gentle breeze
- the sun on your skin
- the feeling of your feet on the ground.
- be aware of your body posture.
- Get curious about any tension and tightness in your muscles, and see if you can let it melt away on the next exhalation.
- You may be curious to see if there is anything you can taste:
- If you live by the ocean there may be salt in the air that you can taste on your lips.
- Now, if they have been closed, open your eyes.
- You may notice the colours look more vivid after this exercise.
- Explore the colours around you.
- Discover what you can see that often goes unobserved: a rainbow, clouds, the movement of the leaves in the wind, a bird in the sky, a butterfly or crawling insect.
- Discover with curiosity at least five different unusual things you can observe.

If you would like to listen to a **recorded version of these mindful activities**, please go to my YouTube channel **Danielle Aitken Clinical Hypnotherapist** and Author.

DAILY MEDITATION PRACTICES

BEGINNER PRACTICES

In this section I have detailed a few examples of simple meditation techniques to spark your interest.

Start with the easy practices and when you become used to those, you might like to try some of the more advanced techniques. With practice you can gain enormous benefit from spending as little as one minute several times a day.

There are many wonderful books, courses, apps, and types of meditations available. Again, I will say I am not here to reinvent the wheel, merely to suggest that there is probably a practice that's right for you. I invite you to get curious, explore and see what works for you.

For short breath meditations that can be done in as little as one minute, refer to ***Helpful breath practices.***

. . .

For guided progressive muscle relaxation, and my guided Heart Coherence meditation and other helpful techniques, please go to my YouTube Channel: ***Danielle Aitken Clinical Hypnotherapist***

WALKING MINDFUL MEDITATION

Take yourself to a place in nature or just begin where you are at this moment. Either is fine. As with all practices we will use the breath to get centred and grounded in the present moment.

STEPS

- Allow your breath to slow and deepen.
- Pay particular attention to the exhalation and allow it to comfortably lengthen.
- As you release the exhalation, allow the shoulders to drop and release any muscular tension you have been holding in your body.
- Feel your feet on the ground as you notice the position of your body and gently and comfortably straighten and align your posture.
- Become aware of where you are and what is around you; the sights, smells, sounds and sensations.
- Now you are ready to begin mindfully walking.
- Be aware of the act of lifting your foot, moving it forward and placing it in front of you.
- Listen for the repetitive sound of placing your foot on the surface on which you are walking.
- Walk at a pace that feels right to you.
- You may choose to count your steps as you walk or count the breath as you breathe in and out. The repetitive nature of the count is very meditative.

- Allow your awareness to expand to notice all that is around you.
- Notice with curiosity and interest what you can see, hear, feel and smell.
- Allow your focus of attention to be fully in the present moment.
- Continue walking in full awareness for as long as feels comfortable.
- When you are ready to halt your practice, simply stop walking, take another deep and mindful breath as you allow your awareness to come back to your body and notice how good you feel.

CANDLE GAZE MEDITATION

This is a great meditation for parents to do with children.

It involves fixing the attention on an object, in this case the candle flame.

Always ensure the candle is safely placed to enable stability and to avoid any contact with other surfaces.

STEPS

- Take a moment to prepare your environment.
- You may like to close the blinds and soften the lighting.
- Find a sitting position of comfort where you will be undisturbed for ten – fifteen minutes
- Position the candle at arm's length at approximately eye level.
- Allow your eyes to close for one minute as you focus on

your breath, releasing any muscular tension from your body.
- Open your eyes and allow your full attention to be directed to the candle flame.
- Observe the flame without blinking, however if you feel you need to blink, do so, then redirect your attention back to the flame.
- If other thoughts come to mind, notice them without judgement and allow your attention to return to the flame.
- You can use your imagination to imagine the flame represents warmth, love, or self-acceptance.
- Allow yourself to sit with the candle gaze focus for ten – fifteen minutes.
- At the completion of your meditation, safely extinguish the flame.

GRATITUDE MEDITATION

Start by focusing your attention on the many things you have in your life to be grateful for.

For example, 'I am grateful for …' my warm bed, a cup of coffee, clean running water, a loving friend or spouse, warm slippers, food on the table, my favourite place in nature, a loving pet.

There is so much to be grateful for, but the last step in this meditation goes beyond thinking, as you connect to the *feelings* of gratitude, and this is where the magic happens.

According to the HeartMath institute, when you connect to the feeling of gratitude your body begins to release 1400 beneficial chemicals and hormones directly into your blood stream. The wonderful healing, rejuvenating and immune boosting effects connecting to the feelings of gratitude can last in the body for up to six hours! Now that's impressive, so why not give this one a try?

STEPS

- Find a place of comfort where you will not be disturbed.
- Turn off distracting devices for the duration of this practice.
- Close your eyes and allow your focus to go to the breath.
- Allow the breath to slow and deepen.
- Extend the exhalation so it is twice as long as the inhalation and relax into the exhalation.
- You may like to place your focus on your heart.
- Now allow those things you are grateful for to filter through your awareness.
- Focus on the feeling of gratitude, really connect to the *feeling* and notice how you feel in your body when you embrace this gratitude feeling.
- Hold this feeling for as long as you can.
- Expand the feeling as you continue to feel gratitude for all those things in your life that you are grateful for.

YOUR THOUGHTS ARE POWERFUL
Challenging Unhelpful Thoughts

PATTERN INTERRUPT

STEP 1: Bring the thought into conscious awareness

- I'm aware I'm having that thought **again**....

Note: The use of the word 'again' is important here, as it is a reminder that these are repetitive thoughts that you have probably thought many times before.

Now you *are* aware! As soon as you are aware of anything, you always get to choose what to do next. This position of choice puts you in the driver's seat. What you choose to do next *will* determine your outcomes.

STEP 2 : Challenging the thought

- Is this a real thought?

- Is it based on fear or fact?
- Have I thought it many times before?
- Will I benefit from listening to it again?
- Whose words are these; do they belong to me or someone else who has criticised me in the past?
- If I believe these thoughts, will this take me toward where I want to be, or away from it?

The bottom line is, if you only ask yourself one question it should be:

Is believing or focusing on this thought or feeling helpful?

If the answer to the last question is NO, it is time to release your hold on the thought or feeling, and let it go without judgement.

HOW?

You can use your powerful imagination to push it away, or let it simply pass you by, in any way that works best for you.

Some possibilities are to imagine the thought to be like:

- Leaves on the stream floating away from you
- Clouds in the sky drifting past you
- Trains of thought pulling out of the station while you stand on the platform.

LETTING GO

- Put the thought in the bin and shut the lid.
- Lock it in a cupboard and throw away the key.
- Flush it away.

- Fade it out like an old photo.
- Pixilate it away.
- Turn your back on it and walk away.
- Imagine it to be like a balloon drifting toward the horizon, fading out of sight and out of mind.

The possibilities here are endless. Choose an option that works for you.

How else can we challenge unhelpful thoughts?

The simple act of changing the way you think and speak about the issue is also helpful.

Statements such as those listed below, can respectfully be challenged by changing the way you think, speak, and feel about these issues.

- I have anxiety.
- I have depression.
- I'm not confident.

These can be replaced with more helpful statements such as

- I sometimes have anxious or depressed feelings and thoughts.
- I don't feel confident about that task.

This reframe, helps to remind us that we are not our thoughts and we are not our feelings.

You were you, before these thoughts and feelings came to mind, and you will be you long after they have gone.

STEP 3 Redirect your attention to the present moment by using the breath, then change your focus.

- Take a breath and return to the present moment.
- Focus your attention on the exhalation as you simultaneously relax your body releasing any tightness from those places you hold tension in your body:
- shoulders / neck / chest.
- Notice how you can relax more and more with each exhalation.

Remember these thoughts will probably return, as you have been in the habit of focusing on them. This is okay, but your mission is to interrupt the pattern as soon as you are aware, by practicing these steps.

The more you run this new pattern, the more you will be creating new neural connections that will lead to new neural pathways for a different way of thinking and feeling. Remember Hebb's Rule: *Neurons that fire together wire together*

Once you have changed the focus from the problematic thoughts or feelings, and have stepped out of stress mode by using the breath to ground yourself in the present moment, now is a great time to change your focus to your solution state.

Your solution state is 'you' when the old problem no longer exists.

If the problem was, 'I feel anxious', the solution may be to focus on you feeling calm and in control.

If the problem was, 'I feel afraid', the solution is to focus on feeling safe and all that feeling safe entails.

Take a moment to really consider what your solution state may look like feel like and be like. How will you know you have achieved it? What will you be doing? What will you no longer be doing?

∼

Please refer to: ***Creating Your Solution State***

CREATING YOUR SOLUTION STATE

Connecting to the powerful subconscious mind

THE CURRENT PROBLEM

- anxiety
- I can't work
- low self esteem
- I'm never good enough
- I can't get my message across
- tension in my body
- tightness in the chest
- mental fog
- constant pain
- heavy feelings weighing me down
- everything feels unsafe
- darkness

YOUR GOAL or SOLUTION
You when the problem no longer exists

- calm
- being productive
- proud of myself
- happy being me
- communicating well
- being heard
- relief
- comfortable in my skin
- clarity
- relaxed, comfortable body
- at peace
- like a weight has lifted
- feeling safe
- light and bright

STEPS

- Think about your old problem and all it entails.
- You may choose to do this on a piece of paper.
- Draw a line down the middle of your paper, dividing it in two.
- Place anything that is part of the problem on the left side of the page. Place anything that is a part of your solution on the right side of the page.
- The questions below may help you identify all aspects of your problem and your solution.
- Be very detailed here.

PROBLEM:

- How does the problem make you feel, act, behave, and think?
- What does the problem allow you to do, what does it prevent you from doing?
- Have you tried to keep it a secret?
- Who else knows about the problem, how does this make you feel?
- What are the emotions created by the problem?
- What sensations do you experience?
- Are there any colours connected to it?
- Are there any sounds connected to it?

SOLUTION:

REALLY IMAGINE what life will be like when the problem no longer exists.

- How will you feel?
- What emotions will you be experiencing?
- How will life look?
- What will you be doing?
- What will you no longer be doing?
- Are there any colours connected with this solution state?
- What are the sounds, tastes smells associated with your solution?
- Are there any bodily sensations?
- How will you know your problem no longer exists?

Remember to always use solution state language here.

Your powerful sub-conscious mind knows the problem all too well and will immediately respond to your thoughts if you allow problem language to penetrate your musings.

When you have a very clear image of what your solution state looks like and feels like, take a few deep breaths focusing on the exhalation to relax mind and body.

Really imagine or pretend, however you do this is fine, that you have already achieved your solution and that you are currently living this life.

The amazing powerhouse that is your subconscious mind cannot tell the difference between imagination or reality and will respond as though what you are imagining is real.

You will therefore begin to feel the way you are thinking; more confident, happier, more productive, healthier. The most beneficial part for you is to remember, where the mind goes, the body automatically follows.

According to neuro-scientific research, when you do this visualisation activity, you are creating and strengthening new neural pathways. The more you focus on your new empowered state, according to research, the more these become your dominant pathways and you effectively rewire your brain for your new condition.

DAILY GRATITUDE PRACTICES

FIVE THINGS

This is an effective practice that I give to my clients to start their day off with a positive focus.

As previously mentioned, the thoughts you choose to focus on at the beginning of your day will influence how the rest of your day progresses.

STEPS

- When you wake up in the morning take a few calming breaths.
- Ensure the exhalation is slightly longer than the inhalation.
- Bring to mind at least five things you are grateful for today.

- These can be every day things such as; a warm bed, a cup of coffee, fresh running water, electricity.
- Focus on these things and allow yourself to really feel the gratitude.
- Give thanks.

Research has shown that starting your day with gratitude leads to increased positivity, productivity, and happiness in your day.

WHAT WENT WELL TODAY?

This is a great practice that helps to wire our brains for more positivity.

STEPS

At the end of the day, instead of focusing on what went wrong in your day (as we often do due to our predisposition to notice the negative), try instead discussing what went well.

This is also a great technique to use with children.

Choose your special someone, take time to sit and embrace the concepts of **mindful listening**, whilst you discuss with interest what went well in your day.

GRATITUDE JOURNAL

For those of you who love journaling, this is a wonderful tool to embrace.

Journaling is a very mindful technique that can chronicle your progress, but when used for the practice of acknowledging gratitude, it can be a tangible record of the positive things in your life.

STEPS

Take a few minutes each day to practice journaling the things you are grateful for.

You may choose to sit and take time to really become inquisitive about the things that are often taken for granted;

- the things you already have
- the things that are working for you.

Focus on different aspects of your life each day.

The act of journaling what you are grateful for can benefit relationships and generally improve feelings of appreciation and wellbeing.

GRATITUDE OBJECTS

Many people choose an inanimate object, such as a gratitude stone, a crystal, candle, or other object that can either be held or observed as an anchor or physical reminder to think of gratitude throughout their day.

Each time they see or touch the object throughout their day, they are reminded to think of what they are grateful for. This awareness creates a more positive mindset over time as the person actively goes in search of what is good, and what is working. This is effective in rewiring the brain for more positivity, and in fostering a gratitude mindset.

AFTERWORD

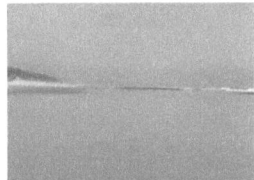

I hope you have found value in what has been presented in this handbook, and that you continue to use these principles to create the lifestyle changes that you desire.

Please be aware that the material presented is in no way an exhaustive list of helpful techniques, merely some that I have found to be effective and useful for both myself and my clients over many years.

I hope that you continue to enjoy practising these principles and techniques every day and perhaps even feel inspired to dive even deeper into the vast sea of information that is currently available on these topics.

Regards Danielle

ABOUT THE AUTHOR

I am passionate about human potential and the ability we have to heal, mind and body

Danielle Aitken

Danielle has worked in the health care sector for forty years, in various capacities: Registered Nurse, Midwife, Counsellor, and Clinical Hypnotherapist. She is also a tutor of clinical hypnotherapy and counselling and is a clinical supervisor to other therapists. As the current National President of the Australian Hypnotherapists' Association, Danielle is passionate about empowering people to achieve their goals and reach their true potential.

Author of *Sarah's Story: Life after IVF* and *The Ripples: What lies Beyond*, both Amazon Best Sellers, Danielle uses her writing to educate, and to create awareness about serious topics, choosing to use the power of the written word to create a vehicle in which to carry these important messages, and in doing so, creating needed conversations.

ALSO BY DANIELLE AITKEN

Author of:

Sarah's Story: Life after IVF

MMH Press 2018 & Project Heart Publishing 2019

The Ripples: What Lies Beyond

Project Heart Publishing, 2020

Invited Author Contributor to the following anthologies:

- **'Dare to Believe'** in *Dance in the fire of life*
- ICK.com llc Publishing House, 2019
- **'Are you Listening now?'** in *The Colours of Me* MMH Press, 2021

"BELIEVE AND YOU WILL ACHIEVE"

WITHIN YOU, RIGHT NOW,
YOU HAVE THE MOST AMAZING ABILITY TO CREATE CHANGE.

THIS ABILITY IS AVAILABLE TO YOU
WHEN THE MIGHT AND TRUE POTENTIAL OF
THE **MIND**, **HEART** AND **BODY** UNITE
IN PERFECT HARMONY'

DANIELLE AITKEN

REFERENCES

- https://greatergood.berkeley.edu/profile/jon_kabat_zinn
- https://www.medicalnewstoday.com/articles/324417
- https://www.medicinenet.com/neuroplasticity/definition.htm
- https://www.emotiv.com/glossary/neuroplasticity/
- https://theconversation.com/what-is-brain-plasticity-and-why-is-it-so-important-55967
- https://www.mindful.org/new-research-on-mindfulness-and-meditation-winter-2020/
- https://positivepsychology.com/benefits-of-mindfulness/
- https://www.livescience.com/65446-sympathetic-nervous-system.html
- https://www.floridamindfulness.org
- https://www.drweil.com/videos-features/videos/breathing-exercises-4-7-8-breath/
- http://webhome.auburn.edu/~mitrege/ENGL2210/USNWR-mind.html
- Stress | Definition of Stress by Merriam-Webster
- https://au.reachout.com/articles/what-stress-does-to-the-body
- https://www.monash.edu/
- https://www.springfieldwellnesscenter.com/
- https://www.karger.com/Article/FullText/510696#:~:text=Allostatic%20load%20was%20linked%20to,peripheral%20arterial%20disease%20%5B244%5D.
- https://positivepsychology.com/benefits-gratitude-research-questions/ 10 health benefits of meditation (ucdavis.edu)

www.ingramcontent.com/pod-product-compliance
Lightning Source LLC
Chambersburg PA
CBHW030301010526
44107CB00053B/1769